Vocabulary Development for ESL Students

—— Advanced Level ——

Lisa Solski

BRIEF OVERVIEW: This workbook teaches Advanced Level ESL students 150 common words to increase conversation, comprehension, and writing. Simple Strategies included incorporate new vocabulary into everyday life situations.

Copyright © On The Mark Press 2017

This publication may be reproduced under licence from Access Copyright, or with the express written permission of On The Mark Press, or as permitted by law. All rights are otherwise reserved, and no part of this publication may be reproduced, stored in a retrieval system, or transmitted in any form or by any means, electronic, mechanical, photocopying, scanning, recording or otherwise, except as specifically authorized.

All Rights Reserved.

Printed in Canada.

Published in Canada by:
On The Mark Press
Belleville, ON
www.onthemarkpress.com

Funded by the Government of Canada

OTM18114   ISBN: 9781770788732 © On The Mark Press

At A Glance

Learning Expectations	Recognizes New Words	Uses a dictionary, thesaurus, and personal dictionary.	Uses flash cards and finds a helper to practise pronunciation.	Divides words into syllables.	Examines root words, prefixes, and suffixes.	Uses context when reading.
Recognizes new vocabulary words when they are presented.	●					
Uses a dictionary, thesaurus and Personal Dictionary to learn new words.		●				
Uses flash cards and finds a helper to practise pronunciation.			●			
Divides words into syllables.				●		
Examines root words, prefixes, and suffixes.					●	
Uses context when reading.						●

Table of Contents

At a Glance 2

Teacher Assessment Rubric. 4

Student Self-Assessment Rubric 5

Acquiring New Vocabulary 6

Follow These Steps for Each Lesson 12

LESSON 1: WEATHER AND CLIMATE VOCABULARY 13

LESSON 2: EMERGENCY VOCABULARY. 18

LESSON 3: WORKPLACE SAFETY VOCABULARY 23

LESSON 4: HOUSEHOLD MAINTENANCE VOCABULARY 28

LESSON 5: MEDICAL PROFESSION VOCABULARY. 33

LESSON 6: COMPUTER VOCABULARY 38

LESSON 7: ELECTRONICS AND TECHNOLOGY VOCABULARY 43

LESSON 8: METRIC WEIGHTS AND MEASURES VOCABULARY 48

LESSON 9: FIRST AID VOCABULARY 53

LESSON 10: OFFICE VOCABULARY. 58

LESSON 11: AUTOMOBILE VOCABULARY 63

LESSON 12: AIRPLANE AND AIR TRAVEL VOCABULARY 68

LESSON 13: TELEPHONE AND TELEPHONE GREETINGS VOCABULARY .73

LESSON 14: RESTAURANT VOCABULARY 78

LESSON 15: ENERGY AND ENVIRONMENTAL VOCABULARY. 83

Answer Key. 88

Teacher Assessment Rubric

Student's Name: _____

Put a check mark ✓ in the box that indicates the student's level of achievement.

Level 1	requires assistance, inconsistent effort, shows limited understanding of concepts
Level 2	requires minimal assistance, shows limited understanding of concepts
Level 3	independent, consistent effort, shows general understanding of concepts
Level 4	independent, consistent effort, shows thorough understanding of concepts

Criteria	Level 1	Level 2	Level 3	Level 4
Recognizes new vocabulary words when they are presented.				
Uses a dictionary, thesaurus and Personal Dictionary to learn new words.				
Uses flash cards and finds a helper to practise pronunciation.				
Divides words into syllables.				
Examines root words, prefixes, and suffixes.				
Uses context when reading.				

Student Self-Assessment Rubric

Name: _____ Date: _____

Put a check mark ✓ in the box that best describes your performance. Then add your points.

Expectations	1 Needs Improvement	2 Sometimes	3 Frequently	4 Always/ almost always	Points
Recognizes new vocabulary words when they are presented.					
Uses a dictionary, thesaurus and Personal Dictionary to learn new words.					
Uses flash cards and finds a helper to practise pronunciation.					
Divides words into syllables.					
Examines root words, prefixes, and suffixes.					
Uses context when reading.					

Acquiring New Vocabulary

Unfamiliar vocabulary prevents English language learners from understanding what they read. Chances are they often ask themselves questions like this when they read.

- What is this word?
- Have I ever seen this word before?
- What are the parts of this word?
- What does this word mean?
- How should I use this word when writing?

This book is designed to help English learners become more successful in understanding and using English words. Experts agree that **reading, writing, speaking and listening** are the keys to developing a better vocabulary. One of the many frustrations students encounter when **reading** new material is unfamiliar vocabulary. It is not uncommon while **reading** a passage for students to come across several unfamiliar words that prevent them from understanding the passage, not to mention the frustration it causes. Then, when **writing**, they have to create ideas and organize them into meaningful phrases, clauses and sentences that others can understand. **Writing** also requires proper punctuation, grammar and spelling. In order to use these essential skills, an acceptable level of vocabulary is needed. When **listening**, students have to pay attention to the words and try to interpret the meanings. Often, this involves several processes happening at once. Finally, when **speaking**, students have to think ahead about how to respond appropriately in conversations. This chart asks students to answer yes or no to these questions.

Rate Yourself

Rate yourself on how you feel about your own English vocabulary. Answer yes or no.

Yes	No	
		Frequently, I encounter words that I cannot pronounce or do not understand.
		Repeating new words and using a dictionary or thesaurus helps improve my vocabulary.
		When my teacher uses pictures, flash cards and other activities, I feel like I am learning new words more easily.
		Using a dictionary helps me to understand new words. It also helps me to see how words are pronounced and broken down into syllables.
		Reading introduces me to new words and helps improve my vocabulary.

Acquiring New Vocabulary

Repetition is Important!

In order to understand new words, it is important to learn and use them. This workbook presents vocabulary words in a repetitious manner and in different contexts. This framework provides an opportunity to use repetition, which is the key. By learning the meanings of words and interacting with them in different ways, students begin to feel more comfortable using the words. After completing a lesson, the words soon become a larger part of the learner's language.

Using the Dictionary and Thesaurus

It is important to use a good dictionary and thesaurus while reading; these tools should be on hand at all times and used when needed. Also, it is very important that the dictionary or thesaurus match the level at which the student is learning-bookstores carry these resource books at various levels and the right level must be chosen. Digital tools are very useful for everyday conversations as they are easily accessible and put students more at ease. Using a dictionary or thesaurus can mean the difference between understanding and not understanding a passage or a conversation. Having these tools on hand makes it possible to look up the word and its meaning immediately without having to wait until later. It is very important that students look up the words themselves rather than relying upon a teacher or another person to explain the meanings to them. In that way, they remember them better. Furthermore, while writing, dictionaries and thesauruses help quickly to improve word choice and to raise vocabulary to a higher level.

Keeping a Personal Dictionary

A personal dictionary can be an easy, invaluable tool in learning new words. It is simply a list of unfamiliar words and their meanings written into a notebook or recorded on the computer. When learning new vocabulary, it is important to write down new words encountered while reading or speaking, look them up in a dictionary or thesaurus and organize them in a meaningful way. Grouping words according to root words, prefixes and suffixes is one useful way of learning new words. By adding words to lists and reviewing the formats on a regular basis, learners become more familiar with the way in which patterns interact to help them become more successful at using vocabulary.

Flash Cards Can Help

Flash Cards are an excellent way to learn new vocabulary: making and using flashcards is a fast, efficient way to learn new vocabulary. The new word goes on one side and the meaning goes on the other side—together they form a useful way to record, practise and learn new vocabulary. Writing a sentence to accompany the words helps, and it is easy to review the cards as part of daily routines: on the bus, during lunch breaks, etc.

Find Mentors or Other Helpers!

It is very important to practise new skills every day, and it does not have to happen alone. Finding a learning partner or mentor is an ideal way to practise vocabulary and build confidence. Also, when learners are given opportunities in class to interact with each other in this way learning happens even more easily. If needed, tutors can help as well. There are several other ways to build vocabulary such as volunteering for organizations and businesses at jobs that require conversation. These methods quickly provide rewards in learning and take place in a natural setting. They provide the learner with valuable opportunities to use the English language to improve speaking, and enhance vocabulary. Public libraries frequently offer conversation classes, as well, in which people can simply get together with others to practise English.

Practising Clear Speech

There are many ways to practise pronunciation, and it is important to recognize that clear speech is extremely important. At home, reading aloud and recording articles from text or online sources and reviewing the recordings to make changes helps learners speak more effectively. Online websites are great places to learn more effective speech through listening and practising important sounds and phrases. It is a great way to learn alone or in groups. Some websites are very advanced and allow students to listen, read, record, receive feedback and practise in unique ways.

Reading For Thirty Minutes Daily Is Essential

One of the most effective ways to learn new vocabulary is by reading regularly, and frequently. Busy students benefit by setting aside thirty minutes at the end of the day for reading. The internet is the preferred method of reading today, and there are several websites with reading material geared to teaching new vocabulary. These websites contain a variety of formats including novels, short stories, poems, news articles, etc. Moreover, tackling new information while learning is also beneficial.

Acquiring New Vocabulary

Summarizing and paraphrasing the main ideas and key points while reading helps tremendously. By setting aside a short period of time each day to read, learners will soon begin to reap the benefits.

Syllabication

The vowels are **a, e, i, o** and **u**. Sometimes, **y** and **w** are also considered vowel sounds. Syllables are the sounds heard when these words are pronounced, and they contain separate sounds. The number of syllables in a word is the number of times the listener hears a vowel sound. For example, in the word **dog**, there is one syllable—the sound of the short vowel **o**. In the word **puppy**, there are two syllables—the sound of the short vowel **u** and the sound of the vowel sound **y** (pronounced **long- e**). Dictionaries separate words into syllables using hyphens or dots. Dividing new words into syllables while reading is a helpful exercise not to be overlooked. It is amazing how quickly new words can become part of everyday vocabulary by practising this activity.

To Divide Words into Syllables:

- Divide words after prefixes: un-clean;
- Divide words before suffixes: express-ing;
- Divide words between double consonants: fos-sil;
- For words with long vowel sounds, divide after the vowel: slo-gan;
- For words with short vowel sounds: divide after the consonant: sev-en.

Prefixes/ Suffixes/Root Words

Prefixes

Prefixes are letters or groups of letters added to the beginnings of words; they change the meanings of the words. Common prefixes are **re, ex,** and **pre**. For example, learners probably use the word **redo** frequently. What does **redo** mean? By breaking the word into syllables, it can be seen that **do** means to perform an activity. By adding the prefix **re**, which means **to do again**, the meaning changes. It is evident that knowing the meaning of a prefix and the root word, can help in figuring out the meanings of many new words. Other widely used prefixes include **un, in** and **dis**.

Suffixes

Suffixes are letters or groups of letters that appear at the endings of words. Like prefixes, suffixes change the meanings of words. Furthermore, as a suffix is added to a word, the word changes from one format or part of speech to another. For example, the suffix **ment** means a state of being or particular place. By adding **ment** to the verb establish, the word establishment results, which means a location where people carry out different procedures. Common suffixes include ***ment, tion, ly***. By taking time to break words down into words and suffixes, they are easier to learn, use and remember.

Root Words

Root words are the main or basic parts of words, and these basic parts contain the meanings of the words. For example, the root word **care** means having or showing concern. Other words develop from this basic word such as careful, careless and carefully. Sometimes, words contain more than one root word such as popcorn (pop and corn) and fireman (fire and man). Since root words contain the meaning of words, it is important to use these roots to help unlock the meaning of other words. Students will be amazed at the number of words they can add to their vocabularies by studying root words and their meanings. Grammar books and online sources often contain lists of root words and their meanings that help learners acquire this skill. It quickly helps with the identification of the meanings of many words and recognizes the relationships with other languages, as well.

Learning Words From Context

Using context means using words and sentences situated **close to the sentence in question** to decipher the meaning of a word or expression. By examining the nearby words and sentences, it is possible to figure out the meaning of new words as well as entire sentences. A good strategy is to read through the entire sentence and search for the key words as they are good clues to meaning. Another strategy is to read the sentences before and after the sentence or phrase in question as they also contain meaningful clues. These clues are called context clues. It is good practise to read back at least two sentences and forward at least one sentence while searching for clues.

Now let's practise. Look through this sentence to find the key words as they contain valuable clues to the meaning. Read this sentence. **After paying off all of their credit cards, the young couple felt like a tremendous load had been taken off their shoulders.** By determining the meaning of the word, **tremendous** (massive, huge, monumental), it is possible to see that the sentence means that the young couple feel that the pressure of the credit cards no longer exists.

Acquiring New Vocabulary

Summary:

- Repetition is important, so practise words in different ways.
- Carry and use a dictionary and thesaurus (print or online).
- Make and use flash cards and a personal dictionary.
- Regularly practise clear speech.
- Read on a daily basis.
- Study format: Divide words into syllables, locate root words, prefixes and suffixes of words.

Follow these steps for each lesson.

1. **REPETITION:** Repeat the word aloud several times.

2. **READ:** Read the vocabulary words and definitions.

3. **MATCH:** Match the new word or sentence to the picture.

4. **PERSONAL DICTIONARY:** Create your own personal dictionary. On each page, include:
   a. A dictionary definition
   b. A sample sentence
   c. An original sentence

5. **READ:** Read daily for at least 30 minutes.

6. **PRACTISE:** Examine prefixes, suffixes, and root words, of words and find new words that contain the same patterns.

9. **CONTEXT:** Use context clues to help you learn new words.

10. **DICTIONARY and THESAURUS:** Keep these tools handy, and use them frequently.

Lesson 1: Weather and Climate Vocabulary

Look at the illustration. What do you think the word means?

Predict a meaning based on the illustration.

#	Word	Predicted Meaning	Illustration
1.	weather forecast		
2.	Celsius temperature scale		
3.	freezing point		
4.	temperature scale		
5.	wind chill factor		

Lesson 1 Weather and Climate Vocabulary   Name:

#	Word	Predicted Meaning	Illustration
6.	thunderstorm warning		
7.	thunderstorm watch		
8.	lightning flash or lightning strike		
9.	tornado		
10.	relative humidity		

Lesson 1 Weather and Climate Vocabulary   Name:

Find the Meaning:

Match the Vocabulary Words with the meanings. Write the correct letter in the answer column.

#	Vocabulary Words	Answer		Meanings
1.	weather forecast		a.	the temperature at which a liquid becomes a solid
2.	Celsius temperature scale		b.	flashes of light produced when electrical charges move out from the clouds during a storm
3.	freezing point		c.	scale used to measure the heat an object contains
4.	temperature scale		d.	a prediction issued by meteorologists about future weather conditions
5.	wind chill factor		e.	a warning stating that a thunderstorm is very likely to occur
6.	thunderstorm warning		f.	a strong destructive windstorm also called a twister appearing together with a funnel cloud
7.	thunderstorm watch		g.	temperature scale based on a freezing point of 0 degrees and a boiling point of 100 degrees

Lesson 1 Weather and Climate Vocabulary   Name:

#	Vocabulary Words	Answer	Meanings
8.	lightning flash or lightning strike		h. a warning stating that a thunderstorm is possible
9.	tornado		i. the amount of moisture or dampness in the air
10.	relative humidity		j. a factor caused by the wind that makes the skin feel colder than the actual temperature

Congratulations! You have finished this lesson.
Check to see how much you remember.

Circle the best answer.

1. A thunderstorm warning and a thunderstorm watch
    a. refer to exactly the same thing but use different names
    b. refer to different types of weather
    c. refer to the same types of weather but at different levels of warning

2. Freezing is the temperature when
    a. a solid turns into a liquid
    b. a liquid turns into a solid
    c. a liquid turns into a gas

Lesson 1 — Weather and Climate Vocabulary   Name:

Check the Meaning of the Word

Instructions:

Divide each word or words into syllables. Use a dictionary. Then, write a sentence that illustrates the meaning of the word or phrase.

#	Word	Divide the Word into Syllables	Sentence to Illustrate Meaning
1.	weather forecast		
2.	Celsius temperature scale		
3.	freezing point		
4.	temperature scale		
5.	wind chill factor		
6.	thunderstorm warning		
7.	thunderstorm watch		
8.	lightning flash or lightning strike		
9.	tornado		
10.	relative humidity		

Lesson 2

Lesson 2: Emergency Vocabulary

Look at the illustration. What do you think the word means?

Predict a meaning based on the illustration.

#	Word	Predicted Meaning	Illustration
1.	emergency situation		
2.	evacuation order		
3.	power-outage		
4.	gas leak		
5.	chemical spill		

Lesson 2 Emergency Vocabulary   Name:

#	Word	Predicted Meaning	Illustration
6.	explosion		
7.	casualty		
8.	missing person		
9.	flashlight		
10.	911		

Lesson 2 Emergency Vocabulary   Name:

Find the Meaning:

Match the Vocabulary Words with the meanings. Write the correct letter in the answer column.

#	Vocabulary Words	Answer	Meanings
1.	emergency situation		a. a sudden suspension or failure in the supply of electrical power
2.	evacuation order		b. the accidental spilling of hazardous chemicals into the environment
3.	power-outage		c. a serious situation that requires immediate medical or other intervention
4.	gas leak		d. an individual who loses his or her life or suffers badly during an emergency
5.	chemical spill		e. a person who cannot be located
6.	explosion		f. an order issued that requires individuals to go away from a location immediately
7.	casualty		g. small battery-powered light

Lesson 2 Emergency Vocabulary   Name:

#	Vocabulary Words	Answer	Meanings
8.	missing person		h. a sudden eruption of pressure and energy
9.	flashlight		i. leakage of gas that causes a dangerous situation
10.	911		j. the phone number to call in case of an emergency

Congratulations! You have finished this lesson.
Check to see how much you remember.

Answer true or false.

   True   **False**

1. _____   _____   A casualty refers to someone who has been missing for a period of time.

2. _____   _____   During an evacuation, people are removed from a harmful situation such as a flood or fire.

3. _____   _____   9-1-1 is the number to call in emergency situations.

4. _____   _____   A gas leak is the same thing as a chemical spill.

5. _____   _____   During a power-outage, there is no electrical power.

Lesson 2 Emergency Vocabulary Name:

Check the Meaning of the Word

Instructions:

Divide each word or words into syllables. Use a dictionary. Then, write a sentence that illustrates the meaning of the word or phrase.

#	Word	Divide the Word into Syllables	Sentence to Illustrate Meaning
1.	emergency situation		
2.	evacuation order		
3.	power outage		
4.	gas leak		
5.	chemical spill		
6.	explosion		
7.	casualty		
8.	missing person		
9.	flashlight		
10.	911		

Lesson 3: Workplace Safety Vocabulary

Predict the Meaning:

Look at the illustration. What do you think the word means?

Predict a meaning based on the illustration.

#	Word	Predicted Meaning	Illustration
1.	dangerous situation		DANGER (skull and crossbones)
2.	hazardous situation		DANGER HAZARDOUS MATERIALS
3.	emergency exit		Exit sign on door
4.	flammable material		FLAMMABLE (flame symbol)
5.	poisonous substance		POISON (skull and crossbones triangle)

Lesson 3	Workplace Safety Vocabulary	Name:	
#	Word	Predicted Meaning	Illustration
6.	corrosive material		
7.	safety glasses		
8.	safety mask		
9.	safety boots		
10.	hard hat		

Lesson 3 Workplace Safety Vocabulary   Name:

Find the Meaning:

Match the Vocabulary Words with the meanings. Write the correct letter in the answer column.

#	Vocabulary Words	Answer		Meanings
1.	dangerous situation		a.	protective covering made for the face particularly the nose and mouth
2.	hazardous situation		b.	a pair of glasses designed to protect the eyes from damage
3.	emergency exit		c.	a special spot leading outside used only in emergencies
4.	flammable material		d.	a hat worn in the workplace to protect the head from falling objects
5.	poisonous substance		e.	a situation causing danger, harm or possibly death
6.	corrosive material		f.	a substance that contains poison
7.	safety glasses		g.	slow chemical process in which a material wears away or weakens

Lesson 3 Workplace Safety Vocabulary   Name:

#	Vocabulary Words	Answer	Meanings
8.	safety mask		h. a situation in which harm or danger can affect the body
9.	safety boots		i. a material that catches on fire easily
10.	hard hat		j. a pair of boots with steel toes that protect the feet

Congratulations! You have finished this exercise.
Complete the word search using the vocabulary words.

r	t	g	u	p	p	h	n	m	j	o	i
r	k	o	l	x	o	u	h	e	d	c	g
d	f	g	w	r	i	k	d	v	b	n	r
c	o	r	r	o	s	i	v	e	o	p	f
m	n	y	r	e	o	t	y	u	l	k	l
w	t	o	d	a	n	g	e	r	e	r	a
z	f	t	y	u	o	r	u	e	w	s	m
f	r	u	i	o	u	d	s	s	a	w	m
x	c	v	y	u	s	b	c	t	f	d	a
h	a	r	d	h	a	t	e	e	i	g	b
p	g	r	w	q	c	v	f	t	y	x	l
l	h	v	y	c	n	e	g	r	e	m	e

Lesson 3 | Workplace Safety Vocabulary | Name:

Check the Meaning of the Word

Instructions:

Divide each word or words into syllables. Use a dictionary. Then, write a sentence that illustrates the meaning of the word or phrase.

#	Word	Divide the Word into Syllables	Sentence to Illustrate Meaning
1.	dangerous situation		
2.	hazardous situation		
3.	emergency exit		
4.	flammable material		
5.	poisonous substance		
6.	corrosive material		
7.	safety glasses		
8.	safety mask		
9.	safety boots		
10.	hard hat		

Lesson 4: Household Maintenance Vocabulary

Look at the illustration. What do you think the word means?

Predict a meaning based on the illustration.

#	Word	Predicted Meaning	Illustration
1.	leaky toilet		
2.	leaky sink		
3.	refrigerator is not working		
4.	oven is broken		
5.	cable is off		

Lesson 4 — Household Maintenance Vocabulary   Name: _____

#	Word	Predicted Meaning	Illustration
6.	heat is off		
7.	air conditioning is not working		
8.	broken step		
9.	dishwasher is not rinsing		
10.	worn tiles		

Lesson 4 Household Maintenance Vocabulary   Name:

Find the Meaning:

Match the Vocabulary Words with the meanings. Write the correct letter in the answer column.

#	Vocabulary Words	Answer	Meanings
1.	leaky toilet		a. the part of a step or stair where people place their foot is broken
2.	leaky sink		b. the appliance is not keeping the contents cool or cold
3.	refrigerator is not working		c. water is coming out of the sink
4.	oven is broken		d. no heat is coming out of the registers
5.	cable is off		e. the television is not producing a picture
6.	heat is off		f. fluid or water is coming out of a toilet
7.	air-conditioning is not working		g. chamber used for baking is not baking the food

Lesson 4 Household Maintenance Vocabulary   Name:

#	Vocabulary Words	Answer	Meanings
8.	broken step		h. floor or wall tiles are damaged
9.	dishwasher is not rinsing		i. cooling equipment is not keeping the building cool
10.	worn tiles		j. dishwasher is not rinsing the dishes

Congratulations! You have finished this lesson. Use the vocabulary words and phrases to write a conversation between a tenant and landlord. The tenant is A and the landlord is B.

A. _____

B. _____

A. _____

B. _____

A. _____

B. _____

Lesson 4 Household Maintenance Vocabulary   Name:

Check the Meaning of the Word

Instructions:

Divide each word or words into syllables. Use a dictionary. Then, write a sentence that illustrates the meaning of the word or phrase.

#	Word	Divide the Word into Syllables	Sentence to Illustrate Meaning
1.	leaky toilet		
2.	leaky sink		
3.	refrigerator is not working		
4.	oven is broken		
5.	cable is off		
6.	heat is off		
7.	air-conditioning is not working		
8.	broken step		
9.	dishwasher is not rinsing		
10.	worn tiles		

Lesson 5: Medical Profession Vocabulary

Predict the Meaning:

Look at the illustration. What do you think the word means?

Predict a meaning based on the illustration.

#	Word	Predicted Meaning	Illustration
1.	general practitioner		
2.	surgeon		
3.	anesthesiologist		
4.	obstetrician		
5.	chiropractor		

Lesson 5 Medical Profession Vocabulary   Name:

#	Word	Predicted Meaning	Illustration
6.	physical therapist		
7.	cardiologist		
8.	ophthalmologist		
9.	orthopedist		
10.	pediatrician		

Lesson 5 Medical Profession Vocabulary   Name:

Find the Meaning:

Match the Vocabulary Words with the meanings. Write the correct letter in the answer column.

#	Vocabulary Words	Answer	Meanings
1.	general practitioner		a. a medical doctor who gives a patient medicine to stop pain during surgery
2.	surgeon		b. a medical doctor who treats many different illnesses and diseases
3.	anesthesiologist		c. a medical doctor trained to treat foot and toe problems
4.	obstetrician		d. a medical professional trained to treat and manage pain especially in the joints
5.	chiropractor		e. a physician who treats children's illnesses and diseases
6.	physical therapist		f. a surgeon who performs surgeries or operations
7.	cardiologist		g. a medical doctor who treats medical problems of the joints

Lesson 5   Medical Profession Vocabulary   Name:

#	Vocabulary Words	Answer	Meanings
8.	ophthalmologist		h. a doctor who gives medical care to expectant mothers
9.	orthopedist		i. a medical doctor who specializes in heart problems
10.	pediatrician		j. a medical specialist who treats diseases of the eye

Congratulations! You have finished this lesson. Circle the word that is misspelled in each line. Then, use each word in a sentence using the past perfect tense.

1. general practitioner   surgeon   peditrician
2. cardiologist   orthopedust   chiropractor
3. obstetrician   surgoen   physical therapist

1. _____
2. _____
3. _____
4. _____
5. _____
6. _____
7. _____
8. _____
9. _____

Lesson 5 — Medical Profession Vocabulary

Name:

Check the Meaning of the Word

Instructions:

Divide each word or words into syllables. Use a dictionary. Then, write a sentence that illustrates the meaning of the word or phrase.

#	Word	Divide the Word into Syllables	Sentence to Illustrate Meaning
1.	general practitioner		
2.	surgeon		
3.	anesthesiologist		
4.	obstetrician		
5.	chiropractor		
6.	physical therapist		
7.	cardiologist		
8.	ophthalmologist		
9.	orthopedist		
10.	pediatrician		

Lesson 6

Lesson 6: Computer Vocabulary

Predict the Meaning:

Look at the illustration. What do you think the word means?

Predict a meaning based on the illustration.

#	Word	Predicted Meaning	Illustration
1.	personal computer		
2.	software		
3.	hardware		
4.	Cloud Computing		
5.	laptop computer		

| **Lesson 6** | Computer Vocabulary | | Name: |

#	Word	Predicted Meaning	Illustration
6.	word-processing program		
7.	external mouse		
8.	computer technician		
9.	USB Stick		
10.	printer		

Lesson 6 Computer Vocabulary   Name: _____

Find the Meaning:

Match the Vocabulary Words with the meanings. Write the correct letter in the answer column.

#	Vocabulary Words	Answer	Meanings
1.	personal computer		a. a device that moves the cursor on the computer screen
2.	software		b. pieces of equipment and devices of a computer
3.	hardware		c. data, programs and operating systems of a computer
4.	Cloud Computing		d. a computer used in homes, schools and offices
5.	laptop computer		e. a computer program used for writing and editing documents
6.	word-processing program		f. a portable computer
7.	external mouse		g. accessing computer programs and using them over the internet

Lesson 6 Computer Vocabulary Name:

#	Vocabulary Words	Answer	Meanings
8.	computer technician		h. a small device used for storing computer data that can be inserted into a USB port on the computer
9.	USB Flash Drive		i. an individual who locates and repairs computer problems
10.	printer		j. a machine that copies images from written documents or web pages

Congratulations! You have finished this lesson. Rewrite these sentences using correct capitalization and punctuation.

1. the technician asked have you used this type of software before

2. aren't you going to plug in the mouse angela eric asked

3. i would like to introduce you to the personal computer specialist of this firm the manager remarked

4. are you talking about replacing the software or hardware the technician inquired

5. a new desktop has been purchased to replace the laptop that was damaged

Lesson 6 Computer Vocabulary

Name:

Check the Meaning of the Word

Instructions:

Divide each word or words into syllables. Use a dictionary. Then, write a sentence that illustrates the meaning of the word or phrase.

#	Word	Divide the Word into Syllables	Sentence to Illustrate Meaning
1.	personal computer		
2.	software		
3.	hardware		
4.	Cloud Computing		
5.	laptop computer		
6.	word-processing program		
7.	external mouse		
8.	computer technician		
9.	USB Flash Drive		
10.	printer		

Lesson 7: Electronics and Technology Vocabulary

Predict the Meaning:

Look at the illustration. What do you think the word means?

Predict a meaning based on the illustration.

#	Word	Predicted Meaning	Illustration
1.	cordless phone		
2.	cellular phone		
3.	MP3/Ipod		
4.	printer/scanner & fax machine		
5.	E-Reader		

Lesson 7 Electronics and Technology Vocabulary   Name:

#	Word	Predicted Meaning	Illustration
6.	text messaging		
7.	ear phones		
8.	digital camera		
9.	LCD television		
10.	virtual reality glasses		

Lesson 7 — Electronics and Technology Vocabulary   Name:

Find the Meaning:

Match the Vocabulary Words with the meanings. Write the correct letter in the answer column.

#	Vocabulary Words	Answer	Meanings
1.	cordless phone		a. a small portable device that plays music
2.	cellular phone		b. a camera that operates electronically and stores the images on memory cards
3.	MP3-Ipod		c. tiny devices placed in the ears for listening to voices or music
4.	printer/scanner & fax machine		d. a telephone that operates without using a cord
5.	E-Reader		e. typing and sending messages on a cell phone
6.	text messaging		f. a small device containing electronic versions of books and other written material
7.	ear phones		g. a phone that can be used in most locations to send and receive calls and perform other tasks

Lesson 7 Electronics and Technology Vocabulary   Name:

#	Vocabulary Words	Answer	Meanings
8.	digital camera		h. a machine that scans and prints text, diagrams, photos, and other images and sends and receives fax messages
9.	LCD television		i. a device that uses special lenses and produces two images to add depth perception
10.	virtual reality glasses		j. thin, lightweight television sets that use liquid-crystal display to create images

Congratulations! You have completed this lesson. Complete the chart by writing the root word of the vocabulary words.

Vocabulary Word	Root Word
text-messaging	
virtual reality glasses	
cellular phone	
e-reader	
printer	

Lesson 7 Electronics and Technology Vocabulary   Name:

Check the Meaning of the Word

Instructions:

Divide each word or words into syllables. Use a dictionary. Then, write a sentence that illustrates the meaning of the word or phrase.

#	Word	Divide the Word into Syllables	Sentence to Illustrate Meaning
1.	cordless phone		
2.	cellular phone		
3.	MP3-Ipod		
4.	printer/scanner & fax machine		
5.	E-Reader		
6.	text messaging		
7.	ear phones		
8.	digital camera		
9.	LCD television		
10.	virtual reality glasses		

Lesson 8

Lesson 8: Metric Weights and Measures Vocabulary

Predict the Meaning:

Look at the illustration. What do you think the word means?

Predict a meaning based on the illustration.

#	Word	Predicted Meaning	Illustration
1.	gram		
2.	kilogram		
3.	litre		
4.	ml		
5.	metre		

48   OTM18114   ISBN: 9781770788732 © On The Mark Press

Lesson 8 — Metric Weights and Measures Vocabulary   Name:

#	Word	Predicted Meaning	Illustration
6.	kilometre		
7.	centimetre		
8.	perpendicular lines		
9.	parallel lines		
10.	hypotenuse		$AB = 15; BC = 8$ $h = ?$

Lesson 8 Metric Weights and Measures Vocabulary   Name:

Find the Meaning:

Match the Vocabulary Words with the meanings. Write the correct letter in the answer column.

#	Vocabulary Words	Answer	Meanings
1.	gram		a. a metric unit equal to 1000 millilitres used to measure capacity
2.	kilogram		b. a metric unit equal to 1/1000 of a litre used for measuring capacity
3.	litre		c. a metric unit equal to 1000 grams used to measure weight
4.	millilitre		d. a metric measurement equal to 1/1000 of a kilogram used to measure weight
5.	metre		e. a metric unit of length equal to 1000 metres used to measure length
6.	kilometre		f. a metric unit equal to 1/100 of a metre used to measure length
7.	centimetre		g. a metric unit equal to 100 cm

Lesson 8 — Metric Weights and Measures Vocabulary   Name:

#	Vocabulary Words	Answer	Meanings
8.	perpendicular lines		h. lines located at 90-degree angles to each other
9.	parallel lines		i. lines at equal distances from each other running in the same direction
10.	hypotenuse		j. a side of a right-angled triangle that lies opposite to the right angle

Congratulations! You have completed this lesson.
Create interesting classified ads using these word pairs.

perpendicular/parallel:

_____

_____

_____

kilometre/litre:

_____

_____

_____

_____

Lesson 8 Metric Weights and Measures Vocabulary   Name:

Check the Meaning of the Word

Instructions:

Divide each word or words into syllables. Use a dictionary. Then, write a sentence that illustrates the meaning of the word or phrase.

#	Word	Divide the Word into Syllables	Sentence to Illustrate Meaning
1.	gram		
2.	kilogram		
3.	litre		
4.	millilitre		
5.	metre		
6.	kilometre		
7.	centimetre		
8.	perpendicular lines		
9.	parallel lines		
10.	hypotenuse		

Lesson 9

Lesson 9: First Aid Vocabulary

Predict the Meaning:

Look at the illustration. What do you think the word means?

Predict a meaning based on the illustration.

#	Word	Predicted Meaning	Illustration
1.	bleeding		
2.	choking		
3.	pulse rate		
4.	CPR		
5.	first aid kit		

Lesson 9 First Aid Vocabulary   Name:

#	Word	Predicted Meaning	Illustration
6.	Heimlich maneuver		
7.	broken leg		
8.	dislocated kneecap		
9.	poisoning		
10.	food poisoning		

Lesson 9 — First Aid Vocabulary   Name: _____

Find the Meaning:

Match the Vocabulary Words with the meanings. Write the correct letter in the answer column.

#	Vocabulary Words	Answer	Meanings
1.	bleeding		a. not able to breathe because the air supply is blocked
2.	choking		b. an emergency procedure in which someone breathes air into a victim's mouth and pushes in his/her chest to assist in breathing
3.	pulse rate		c. the kneecap is pushed out of the joint due to an injury or fall
4.	CPR		d. losing blood from the body due to a cut or wound
5.	first aid kit		e. an emergency procedure in which someone pushes on a person's stomach to force out an object that is blocking the breathing tube
6.	Heimlich maneuver		f. a vibration or beat produced when blood flows through the body
7.	broken leg		g. a bag or box containing band-aids, bandages and other equipment

Lesson 9 First Aid Vocabulary   Name:

#	Vocabulary Words	Answer	Meanings
8.	dislocated kneecap		h. becoming ill or dying after eating food containing harmful bacteria
9.	poisoning		i. swallowing a poisonous or toxic substance
10.	food poisoning		j. one or more bones broken in the leg due to an injury

Congratulations! You have completed this lesson. Create a 9-1-1 conversation between a 9-1-1 operator and a caller on the line. Use as many of the vocabulary words from this lesson as you can.

A. _____
B. _____
A. _____
B. _____
A. _____
B. _____
A. _____
B. _____
A. _____
B. _____

Lesson 9 First Aid Vocabulary Name:

Check the Meaning of the Word

Instructions:

Divide each word or words into syllables. Use a dictionary. Then, write a sentence that illustrates the meaning of the word or phrase.

#	Word	Divide the Word into Syllables	Sentence to Illustrate Meaning
1.	bleeding		
2.	choking		
3.	pulse rate		
4.	CPR		
5.	first aid kit		
6.	Heimlich maneuver		
7.	broken leg		
8.	dislocated kneecap		
9.	poisoning		
10.	food poisoning		

Lesson 10

Lesson 10: Office Vocabulary

Predict the Meaning:

Look at the illustration. What do you think the word means?

Predict a meaning based on the illustration.

#	Word	Predicted Meaning	Illustration
1.	photocopier		
2.	conference room		
3.	administrative assistant		
4.	receptionist		
5.	presentation skills		

Lesson 10 — Office Vocabulary   Name:

#	Word	Predicted Meaning	Illustration
6.	docking station		
7.	Human Resources		
8.	staff room		
9.	lock up the office		
10.	confidential		

Lesson 10 Office Vocabulary   Name:

Find the Meaning:

Match the Vocabulary Words with the meanings. Write the correct letter in the answer column.

#	Vocabulary Words	Answer	Meanings
1.	photocopier		a. an office room where business meetings take place
2.	conference room		b. the employee who greets customers or takes phone calls and messages
3.	administrative assistant		c. a machine used for making copies of printed documents such as letters
4.	receptionist		d. an employee who assists a manager or other executive in running a business
5.	presentation skills		e. a department that hires and fires employees
6.	docking station		f. skills related to speaking in front of groups
7.	Human Resources		g. a room where staff members drink coffee or eat lunch

Lesson 10 — Office Vocabulary   Name:

#	Vocabulary Words	Answer	Meanings
8.	staff room		h. information that must be kept private
9.	lock up the office		i. a flat surface used to attach a computer
10.	confidential		j. checking to make sure the office is locked up before leaving for the day

Congratulations! You have completed this lesson. Pretend you are writing a resume. Use these words in sentences you could place on your resume.

1. photocopier _____

_____

2. administrative assistant_____

_____

3. receptionist _____

_____

4. confidential _____

_____

Lesson 10 — Office Vocabulary — Name:

Check the Meaning of the Word

Instructions:

Divide each word or words into syllables. Use a dictionary. Then, write a sentence that illustrates the meaning of the word.

#	Word	Divide the Word into Syllables	Sentence to Illustrate Meaning
1.	photocopier		
2.	conference room		
3.	administrative assistant		
4.	receptionist		
5.	presentation skills		
6.	docking station		
7.	Human Resources		
8.	staff room		
9.	lock up the office		
10.	confidential		

Lesson 11: Automobile Vocabulary

Predict the Meaning:

Look at the illustration. What do you think the word means?

Predict a meaning based on the illustration.

#	Word	Predicted Meaning	Illustration
1.	spare tire		
2.	defroster		
3.	emergency brake		
4.	speedometer		
5.	odometer		

Lesson 11 Automobile Vocabulary   Name:

#	Word	Predicted Meaning	Illustration
6.	ignition		
7.	temperature gauge		
8.	accelerator		
9.	alternator		
10.	radiator		

64

Lesson 11 Automobile Vocabulary   Name:

Find the Meaning:

Match the Vocabulary Words with the meanings. Write the correct letter in the answer column.

#	Vocabulary Words	Answer	Meanings
1.	spare tire		a. a device that cools the engine of a vehicle or other means of transportation
2.	defroster		b. a special brake used to stop a vehicle if the regular brake fails
3.	emergency brake		c. an instrument that records the speed at which a vehicle is travelling
4.	speedometer		d. an instrument that can be turned up or down to control the temperature of a vehicle
5.	odometer		e. a device used to thaw or remove ice from the windshields and keep them clear
6.	ignition		f. an instrument that measures the distance a vehicle has travelled
7.	temperature gauge		g. a device used to cause the engine of a vehicle to start working

Lesson 11   Automobile Vocabulary   Name:

#	Vocabulary Words	Answer	Meanings
8.	accelerator		h. an instrument on the floor of a vehicle that causes the vehicle to go faster
9.	alternator		i. an extra tire
10.	radiator		j. a device that helps to give an electric charge to the battery of a vehicle

Congratulations! You have completed this lesson. Put parenthesis around each noun clause in each sentence.

1. Whoever applies the emergency brake will automatically fail the driving test.
2. She couldn't remember where the spare tire was.
3. The radiator was repaired by whoever had the best qualifications.
4. Sparks coming from the radiator indicate it is overheating.

Explain the term 'noun clause'. Write a sentence of your own containing a noun clause.

_____

_____

_____

_____

Lesson 11 Automobile Vocabulary Name:

Check the Meaning of the Word

Instructions:

Divide each word or words into syllables. Use a dictionary. Then, write a sentence that illustrates the meaning of the word.

#	Word	Divide the Word into Syllables	Sentence to Illustrate Meaning
1.	spare tire		
2.	defroster		
3.	emergency brake		
4.	speedometer		
5.	odometer		
6.	ignition		
7.	temperature gauge		
8.	accelerator		
9.	alternator		
10.	radiator		

Lesson #

Lesson 12: Airplane and Air Travel Vocabulary

Predict the Meaning:

Look at the illustration. What do you think the word means?

Predict a meaning based on the illustration.

#	Word	Predicted Meaning	Illustration
1.	board the plane		
2.	carry-on luggage		
3.	fasten seat belt sign		
4.	call button		
5.	oxygen mask		

Lesson 12 — Airplane and Air Travel Vocabulary

Name:

#	Word	Predicted Meaning	Illustration
6.	metal detector		
7.	air sickness bag		
8.	flight attendant		
9.	boarding pass		
10.	conveyor belt		

Lesson 12 Airplane and Air Travel Vocabulary   Name:

Find the Meaning:

Match the Vocabulary Words with the meanings. Write the correct letter in the answer column.

#	Vocabulary Words	Answer	Meanings
1.	board the plane		a. small bags or suitcases passengers carry on the plane with them
2.	carry-on luggage		b. a sign the pilot uses to tell passengers to keep their seatbelts fastened
3.	fasten seat belt sign		c. device used to locate harmful or dangerous objects
4.	call button		d. a small facial covering passengers place over their faces to obtain oxygen during an emergency
5.	oxygen mask		e. to leave the airport gate area and get on the plane
6.	metal detector		f. a button that passengers push when they need assistance from a flight attendant
7.	air sickness bag		g. an employee who attends to safety and other needs of passengers during an airplane flight

Lesson 12 Airplane and Air Travel Vocabulary   Name:

#	Vocabulary Words	Answer	Meanings
8.	flight attendant		h. a movable belt on which passengers' place items to be checked for security purposes
9.	boarding pass		i. a piece of paper that passengers must present at the gate in order to get on the plane
10.	conveyor belt		j. a bag used in case of air sickness

Congratulations! You have completed this lesson. Complete a conversation between an airline clerk and a passenger boarding a plane. Use as many vocabulary words as you can.

1. _____

2. _____

3. _____

4. _____

5. _____

Lesson 12 Airplane and Air Travel Vocabulary   Name:

Check the Meaning of the Word

Instructions:

Divide each word or words into syllables. Use a dictionary. Then, write a sentence that illustrates the meaning of the word.

#	Word	Divide the Word into Syllables	Sentence to Illustrate Meaning
1.	board the plane		
2.	carry-on luggage		
3.	fasten seat belt sign		
4.	call button		
5.	oxygen mask		
6.	metal detector		
7.	air sickness bag		
8.	flight attendant		
9.	boarding pass		
10.	conveyor belt		

Lesson 13: Telephone and Telephone Greetings Vocabulary

Predict the Meaning:

Look at the illustration. What do you think the word means?

Predict a meaning based on the illustration.

#	Word	Predicted Meaning	Illustration
1.	hello		
2.	goodbye		
3.	thank you		
4.	May I please take a message?		

Lesson 13 Telephone and Telephone Greetings Vocabulary   Name:

#	Word	Predicted Meaning	Illustration
5.	He or she is out of the office.		
6.	He or she is not available to come to the phone.		
7.	Voicemail		
8.	Please repeat that.		
9.	May I place you on hold?		
10.	I am returning your call.		

Lesson 13 Telephone and Telephone Greetings Vocabulary Name:

Find the Meaning:

Match the Vocabulary Words with the meanings. Write the correct letter in the answer column.

#	Vocabulary Words	Answer	Meanings
1.	hello		a. not able to come to the phone
2.	goodbye		b. politely thanking the caller
3.	thank you		c. a greeting used to begin a phone conversation
4.	May I please take a message?		d. away from the office at the time
5.	He or she is out of the office.		e. a word used to end a phone conversation
6.	He or she is not available to come to the phone.		f. obtaining information from a caller to give to another employee
7.	voicemail		g. please say that again.

Lesson 13 Telephone and Telephone Greetings Vocabulary   Name:

#	Vocabulary Words	Answer	Meanings
8.	please repeat that		h. a device that records messages
9.	May I place you on hold?		i. calling a person who has called or left a message
10.	I am returning your call		j. a feature that allows the caller to wait briefly on the phone

Congratulations! You have completed this lesson. Write the vocabulary words in alphabetical order on the lines below.

_____

_____

_____

_____

_____

_____

_____

Lesson 13 Telephone and Telephone Greetings Vocabulary   Name:

Check the Meaning of the Word

Instructions:

Divide each word or words into syllables. Use a dictionary. Then, write a sentence that illustrates the meaning of the word.

#	Word	Divide the Word into Syllables	Sentence to Illustrate Meaning
1.	hello		
2.	goodbye		
3.	thank you		
4.	May I please take a message?		
5.	He or she is out of the office.		
6.	He or she is not available to come to the phone.		
7.	voicemail		
8.	Please repeat that.		
9.	May I place you on hold?		
10.	I am returning your call.		

Lesson 14

Lesson 14: Restaurant Vocabulary

Predict the Meaning:

Look at the illustration. What do you think the word means?

Predict a meaning based on the illustration.

#	Word	Predicted Meaning	Illustration
1.	dining room hostess		
2.	dining room host		
3.	waiter or server		
4.	waitress or server		
5.	grilled		

Lesson 14 Restaurant Vocabulary   Name:

#	Word	Predicted Meaning	Illustration
6.	gratuity		
7.	special of the day		
8.	appetizer		
9.	main course		
10.	dessert à la carte		

Lesson 14 Restaurant Vocabulary   Name:

Find the Meaning:

Match the Vocabulary Words with the meanings. Write the correct letter in the answer column.

#	Vocabulary Words	Answer	Meanings
1.	dining-room hostess		a. female employee who greets and seats customers in a restaurant
2.	dining-room host		b. a form of cooking using fire covered with a frame and metal bars
3.	waiter or server		c. a male employee who greets and seats customers
4.	waitress or server		d. small items of food eaten while waiting for the main course
5.	grilled		e. a male employee who takes orders and serves food in a restaurant
6.	gratuity		f. money left to show appreciation for the server in a restaurant
7.	special of the day		g. a female employee who takes orders and serves food in a restaurant

Lesson 14 Restaurant Vocabulary   Name:

#	Vocabulary Words	Answer	Meanings
8.	appetizer		h. the principal part of the meal
9.	main course		i. ice cream served with the dessert
10.	dessert à la carte		j. a menu item that changes daily, served at a reduced price at times

Congratulations! You have completed this lesson. Choose five words form the vocabulary list. Using vocabulary words, write a recommendation for your favourite restaurant.

_____

_____

_____

_____

_____

_____

_____

_____

Lesson 14 Restaurant Vocabulary   Name:

Check the Meaning of the Word

Instructions:

Divide each word or words into syllables. Use a dictionary. Then, write a sentence that illustrates the meaning of the word.

#	Word	Divide the Word into Syllables	Sentence to Illustrate Meaning
1.	dining room hostess		
2.	dining room host		
3.	waiter or server		
4.	waitress or server		
5.	grilled		
6.	gratuity		
7.	special of the day		
8.	appetizer		
9.	main course		
10.	dessert à la carte		

Lesson 15: Energy and Environmental Vocabulary

Predict the Meaning:

Look at the illustration. What do you think the word means?

Predict a meaning based on the illustration.

#	Word	Predicted Meaning	Illustration
1.	environment		
2.	recycle		
3.	reuse		
4.	energy		
5.	conservation		

Lesson 15 Energy and Environmental Vocabulary   Name:

#	Word	Predicted Meaning	Illustration
6.	air pollution		
7.	radioactivity		
8.	oil sands		
9.	natural gas		
10.	petroleum		

Lesson 15 Energy and Environmental Vocabulary   Name:

Find the Meaning:

Match the Vocabulary Words with the meanings. Write the correct letter in the answer column.

#	Vocabulary Words	Answer	Meanings
1.	environment		a. the physical setting or surroundings
2.	recycle		b. processing materials so they can be used again
3.	reuse		c. following steps in order to prevent the waste or destruction of resources
4.	energy		d. to use materials again
5.	conservation		e. resources used to produce power
6.	air pollution		f. harmful particles given off into the air by the breakdown of atoms
7.	radioactivity		g. dirt, sand and oil found in the ground that is mined to produce fuel

Lesson 15 Energy and Environmental Vocabulary   Name:

#	Vocabulary Words	Answer	Meanings
8.	oil sands		h. giving off impure substances into the air
9.	natural gas		i. gas found below the earth's surface used as fuel
10.	petroleum		j. oil taken from the ground or oil wells and processed into fuel

Congratulations! You have completed this lesson. Write a letter to the editor of a local newspaper expressing your concerns about a recent environmental issue.

_____

_____

_____

_____

_____

_____

_____

Lesson 15 Energy and Environmental Vocabulary Name:

Check the Meaning of the Word

Instructions:

Divide each word or words into syllables. Use a dictionary. Then, write a sentence that illustrates the meaning of the word.

#	Word	Divide the Word into Syllables	Sentence to Illustrate Meaning
1.	environment		
2.	recycle		
3.	reuse		
4.	energy		
5.	consultation		
6.	air pollution		
7.	radioactivity		
8.	oil sands		
9.	natural gas		
10.	petroleum		

Answer Key

ANSWER KEY

LESSON ONE

Find the Meaning:
1.d;   2.g;   3.a;   4.c;   5.j;   6.e;   7.h;   8.b;   9.f;   10.i

Circle the best answer: 1. c 2. b

Check the Meaning of the word:
1. weath-er fore-cast; 2. Cel-si-us scale; 3. freez-ing point ; 4. tem-per-a-ture scale;
5. wind chill fac-tor; 6. thun-der-storm warn-ing; 7. thun-der-storm watch;
8. light-ning strike or light-ning flash; 9. tor-na-do; 10. rel-a-tive hu-mid-i-ty

LESSON TWO

Find the Meaning:
1.c;   2.f;   3.a;   4.i;   5.b;   6.h;   7.d;   8.e;   9.g;   10.j

True-False
1-false; 2-true; 3-true; 4-false; 5-true

Check the meaning of the Word
1. e-mer-gen-cy sit-u-a-tion; 2. e-vac-u-a-tion ord-er; 3. pow-er out-age;
4. gas leak; 5. chem-i-cal spill; 6. ex-plo-sion; 7. cas-u-al-ty; 8. miss-ing per-son;
9. flash-light; 10. di-al 911

LESSON THREE

Find the Meaning:
1.h;   2.e;   3.c;   4.i;   5.f;   6.g;   7.b;   8.a;   9.j;   10.d

Word Search:

r	t	g	u	p	p	h	n	m	j	o	i
r	k	o	l	x	o	u	h	e	d	c	g
d	f	g	w	r	i	k	d	v	b	n	r
c	o	r	r	o	s	i	v	e	o	p	f
m	n	y	r	e	o	t	y	u	l	k	l
w	t	o	d	a	n	g	e	r	e	r	a
z	f	t	y	u	o	r	u	e	w	s	m
f	r	u	i	o	u	d	s	s	a	w	m
x	c	v	y	u	s	b	c	t	f	d	a
h	a	r	d	h	a	t	e	e	i		b
p	g	r	w	q	c	v	f	t	y	x	l
l	h	v	y	c	n	e	g	r	e	m	e

Check the Meaning of the Word:
1. dan-ger-ous sit-u-a-tion; 2. haz-ard-ous sit-u-a-tion; 3. e-mer-gen-cy ex-it;
4. flam-ma-ble ma-te-ri-al; 5. poi-son-ous sub-stance; 6. cor-ro-sive ma-te-ri-al;
7. safe-ty glas-ses; 8. safe-ty mask; 9. safe-ty boots; 10. hard hat

Answer Key

LESSON FOUR
Find the Meaning:
1.f; 2.c; 3.b; 4.g; 5.e; 6.d; 7.i; 8.a; 9.j; 10.h

Check the Meaning of the Word
1. leak-y toi-let; 2. leak-y sink; 3. re-frig-er-a-tor; 4. ov-en is bro-ken; 5. ca-ble is off; 6. heat is off; 7. air con-di-tion-ing is not work-ing; 8. bro-ken step; 9. dish-wash-er is not rins-ing; 10. worn tiles

LESSON FIVE
Find the Meaning:
1.b; 2.f; 3.a; 4.h; 5.g; 6.d; 7.i; 8.j; 9.c; 10.e

Exercise
1. pediatrician
2. orthopedist
3. surgeon

Check the Meaning of the Word
1. gen-er-al prac-ti-tion-er; 2. sur-geon; 3. an-es-the-si-ol-o-gist 4. ob-ste-tri-cian; 5. chi-ro-pract-or; 6. phys-i-cal ther-a-pist; 7. car-di-ol-o-gist; 8. oph-thal-mol-o-gist; 9. or-tho-ped-ist; 10. pe-di-a-tri-cian

LESSON SIX
Find the Meaning
1.d; 2.c; 3.b; 4.g; 5.f; 6.e; 7.a; 8.i; 9.j; 10.h

Exercise
1. The technician asked, "Have you used this type of software before?"
2. "Aren't you going to plug in the mouse, Angela?" Eric asked.
3. "I would like to introduce you to the personal computer specialist of this firm," the manager remarked.
4. "Are you talking about replacing the software or hardware?" the technician inquired.
5. A new desktop has been purchased to replace the laptop that was damaged.

Check the Meaning of the Word
1. per-son-al com-pu-ter; 2. soft-ware; 3. hard-ware; 4. Cloud com-put-ing; 5. lap-top com-put-er; 6. word-pro-cess-ing pro-gram; 7. ex-ter-nal mouse; 8. com-pu-ter tech-ni-cian; 9. USB stick; 10. print-er

LESSON SEVEN
Find the Meaning:
1.d; 2.g; 3.a; 4.h; 5.f; 6.e; 7.c; 8.b; 9.j; 10.i

Exercise
Root Words: text, message; virtue, real, glass; cell, phone; read; Print

Answer Key

Check the Meaning of the Word
1. cord-less phone; 2. cel-lu-lar phone; 3. MP3 I-pod; 4. print-er/scan-ner/fax ma-chine; 5. E-read-er; 6. text mes-sag-ing; 7. ear phones; 8. dig-it-al cam-era; 9. L-C-D tel-e-vi-sion; 10. Vir-tu-al Re-al-i-ty Glasses

LESSON EIGHT
Find the Meaning:
1.d;   2.c;   3.a;   4.b;   5.g;   6.e;   7.f;   8.h;   9.i;   10.j

Check the Meaning of the Word
1. gram; 2. kil-o-gram; 3. li-tre; 4. mil-li-li-tre; 5. me-tre; 6. kil-o-me-tre; 7. cen-ti-me-tre; 8. per-pen-dic-u-lar lines 9. par-al-lel lines; 10. hy-pot-e-nuse

LESSON NINE
Find the Meaning:
1.d;   2.a;   3.f;   4.b;   5.g;   6.e;   7.j;   8.c;   9.i;   10.h

Check the Meaning of the Word
1. bleed-ing; 2. chok-ing; 3. pulse rate ; 4. CPR; 5. first-aid kit; 6. Heim-lich Ma-neu-ver; 7. bro-ken leg; 8. dis-lo-cat-ed knee-cap; 9. poi-son-ing; 10. food poi-son-ing

LESSON TEN
Find the Meaning:
1.c;   2.a;   3.d;   4.b;   5.f;   6.i;   7.e;   8.g;   9.j;   10.h

Check the Meaning of the Word
1. pho-to-cop-i-er; 2. con-fer-ence room; 3. ad-min-is-tra-tive as-sis-tant; 4. re-cep-tion-ist; 5. pres-en-ta-tion skills; 6. dock-ing sta-tion; 7. Hu-man Re-sourc-es; 8. staff room; 9. lock up the of-fice; 10. con-fi-den-tial

LESSON ELEVEN
Find the Meaning:
1.i;   2.e;   3.b;   4.c;   5.f;   6.g;   7.d;   8.h;   9.j;   10.a

Check the Meaning of the Word:
1. spare tire; 2. de-frost-er; 3. e-mer-genc-y brake; 4. speed-om-e-ter; 5. o-dom-e-ter; 6. ig-ni-tion; 7. tem-per-a-ture gauge; 8. ac-cel-er-a-tor; 9. al-ter-na-tor; 10. ra-di-a-tor

LESSON TWELVE
Find the Meaning:
1.e;   2.a;   3.b;   4.f;   5.d;   6.c;   7.j;   8.g;   9.i;   10.h

Check the Meaning of the Word
1. board the plane; 2. car-ry on lug-gage; 3. fas-ten seat belt sign; 4. call but-ton;

5. ox-y-gen; 6. met-al de-tec-tor; 7. air sick-ness bag; 8. flight at-tend-ant; 9. board-ing pass; 10. con-vey-or belt

LESSON THIRTEEN
Find the Meaning:
1.c; 2.e; 3.b; 4.f; 5.d; 6.a; 7.h; 8.g; 9.j; 10.i

Check the Meaning of the Word
1. hel-lo; 2. good-bye; 3. thank-you; 4. May I take a mes-sage please?; 5. He or she is out-of-the of-fice; 6. He or she is not a-vail-a-ble to come to the phone.; 7. voice mail; 8. Could you please re-peat that?; 9. May I place you on hold?; 10. I am re-turn-ing your call

LESSON FOURTEEN
Find the Meaning:
1.a; 2.c; 3.e; 4.g; 5.b; 6.f; 7.j; 8.d; 9.h; 10.i

Check the Meaning of the Word
1. din-ing room host-ess; 2. din-ing room host; 3. wait-er or serv-er; 4. wait-ress or serv-er; 5. grilled; 6. gra-tu-i-ty; 7. Spe-cial of the day; 8. ap-pe-tiz-er; 9. main course; 10. des-sert a la carte

LESSON FIFTEEN
Find the Meaning:
1.a; 2.b; 3.d; 4.e; 5.c; 6.h; 7.f; 8.g; 9.i; 10.j

Check the Meaning of the Word
1. en-vi-ron-ment; 2. re-cy-cle; 3. re-use; 4. en-er-gy; 5. con-sul-ta-tion; 6. air pol-lu-tion; 7. ra-di-o ac-tiv-i-ty; 8. oil sands; 9. nat-u-ral gas; 10. pe-tro-le-um